VIOLIN

101 CLASSICAL THEMES

Available for
FLUTE, CLARINET, ALTO SAX, TENOR SAX, TRUMPET,
HORN, TROMBONE, VIOLIN, VIOLA, CELLO

T0116619

ISBN 978-1-4950-5631-4

HAL•LEONARD®
CORPORATION
7777 W. BLUEMOUND RD. P.O. BOX 13819 MILWAUKEE, WI 53213

In Australia Contact:
Hal Leonard Australia Pty. Ltd.
4 Lentara Court
Cheltenham, Victoria, 3192 Australia
Email: ausadmin@halleonard.com.au

Visit Hal Leonard Online at
www.halleonard.com

CONTENTS

1812 OVERTURE
(Theme)

VIOLIN

PYOTR IL'YICH TCHAIKOVSK~~

Allegro vivace

AIR
from WATER MUSIC

GEORGE FRIDERIC HANDEL

Andante

AIR ON THE G STRING
from ORCHESTRAL SUITE NO. 3

JOHANN SEBASTIAN BACH

ARIOSO
from CANTATA 156

VIOLIN

JOHANN SEBASTIAN BACH

AVE MARIA

based on "Prelude in C Major" by Johann Sebastian Bach

VIOLIN

CHARLES GOUNOD

Moderately

ANDANTE CANTABILE
from STRING QUARTET NO. 1

VIOLIN

PYOTR IL'YICH TCHAIKOVSKY

AVE MARIA

FRANZ SCHUBERT

BIST DU BEI MIR

GOTTFRIED HEINRICH STÖZEL
(previously attributed to J.S. Bach)

AVE VERUM CORPUS

VIOLIN

WOLFGANG AMADEUS MOZART

BADINERIE
from ORCHESTRAL SUITE NO. 2

VIOLIN

JOHANN SEBASTIAN BACH

Quickly, lightly

BARCAROLLE
from THE TALES OF HOFFMANN

VIOLIN

JACQUES OFFENBACH

Moderately

BLUE DANUBE WALTZ

VIOLIN

JOHANN STRAUSS, JR.

Waltz tempo

BOURRÉE IN E MINOR
from LUTE SUITE IN E MINOR

VIOLIN

JOHANN SEBASTIAN BACH

BRANDENBURG CONCERTO NO. 3
(First Movement Theme)

JOHANN SEBASTIAN BACH

BRANDENBURG CONCERTO NO. 5

(First Movement Theme)

JOHANN SEBASTIAN BACH

Moderately

BRIDAL CHORUS
from LOHENGRIN

VIOLIN

RICHARD WAGNER

Moderately

CLAIR DE LUNE
from SUITE BERGAMASQUE

VIOLIN

CLAUDE DEBUSSY

Andante

18

CAN CAN
from ORPHEUS IN THE UNDERWORLD

VIOLIN

JACQUES OFFENBACH

Allegretto moderato

CANON IN D

JOHANN PACHELBEL

Adagio

CARO MIO BEN

TOMMASO GIORDANI

Larghetto

DANCE OF THE HOURS
from LA GIOCONDA

VIOLIN

AMILCARE PONCHIELL

Moderately

DANCE OF THE REED-FLUTES
from THE NUTCRACKER

VIOLIN

PYOTR IL'YICH TCHAIKOVSKY

DANCE OF THE SPIRITS
from ORFEO ED EURIDICE

VIOLIN

CHRISTOPH WILLIBALD VON GLUCK

DANCE OF THE SUGAR PLUM FAIRY
from THE NUTCRACKER

PYOTR IL'YICH TCHAIKOVSKY

EINE KLEINE NACHTMUSIK

(First Movement Theme)

WOLFGANG AMADEUS MOZART

EVENING PRAYER
from HANSEL AND GRETEL

VIOLIN

ENGELBERT HUMPERDINCK

Moderately

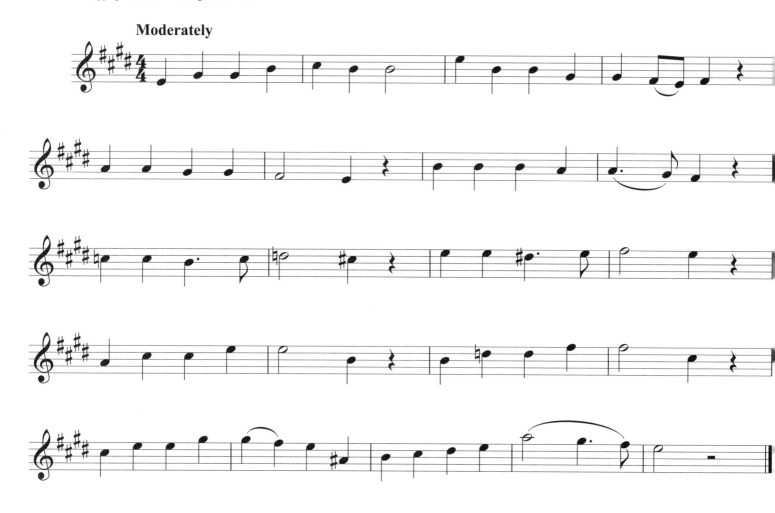

THE FLIGHT OF THE BUMBLEBEE

NICOLAI RIMSKY-KORSAKOV

Vivace

EINE KLEINE NACHTMUSIK

(Second Movement Theme: "Romanze")

VIOLIN

WOLFGANG AMADEUS MOZART

FLOWER DUET

from LAKMÉ

VIOLIN

LÉO DELIBES

Andantino con moto

FUNERAL MARCH
(Marche funèbre)
from PIANO SONATA NO. 2

VIOLIN

FRÉDÉRIC CHOPIN

Lento

FUNERAL MARCH OF A MARIONETTE

VIOLIN

CHARLES GOUNOD

Allegretto

FÜR ELISE
(Bagatelle No. 25)

VIOLIN

LUDWIG VAN BEETHOVEN

THE GREAT GATE OF KIEV
from PICTURES AT AN EXHIBITION

MODEST MUSSORGSKY

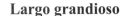

Largo grandioso

GYMNOPÉDIE NO. 1

ERIC SATIE

HABANERA
from CARMEN

VIOLIN

GEORGES BIZET

Allegro quasi andantino

THE HAPPY FARMER
from ALBUM FOR THE YOUNG

VIOLIN

ROBERT SCHUMANN

Brightly, cheerfully

THE HARMONIOUS BLACKSMITH
from HARPSICHORD SUITE NO. 5

GEORGE FRIDERIC HANDEL

Andante

HORNPIPE
from WATER MUSIC

VIOLIN

GEORGE FRIDERIC HANDEL

Allegro maestoso

HUNGARIAN DANCE NO. 5

VIOLIN

JOHANNES BRAHMS

HALLELUJAH CHORUS
from MESSIAH

VIOLIN

GEORGE FRIDERIC HANDEL

INTERMEZZO
from CAVALLERIA RUSTICANA

PIETRO MASCAGNI

JERUSALEM

HUBERT PARRY

IN THE HALL OF THE MOUNTAIN KING

from PEER GYNT

VIOLIN

EDVARD GRIEG

March tempo

JESU, JOY OF MAN'S DESIRING

from CANTATA 147

VIOLIN

JOHANN SEBASTIAN BACH

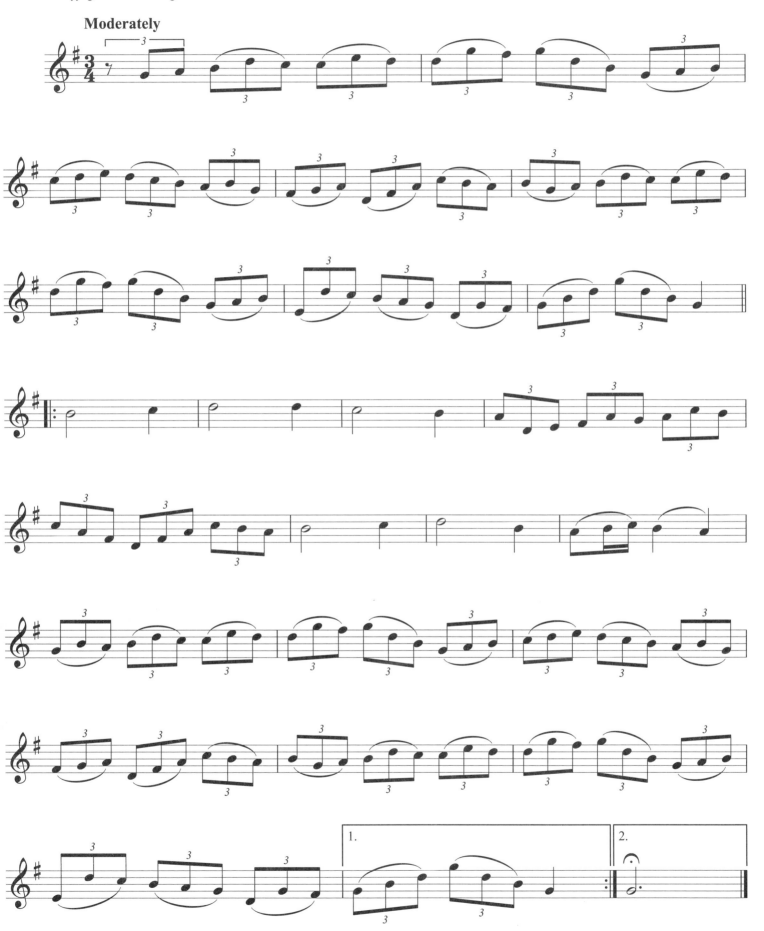

LARGO
from XERXES

VIOLIN

GEORGE FRIDERIC HANDEL

Larghetto

LAUDATE DOMINUM
from VESPERAE SOLENNES DE CONFESSORE

VIOLIN

WOLFGANG AMADEUS MOZART

LULLABY
(Wiegenlied)

VIOLIN

JOHANNES BRAHMS

Moderately, tenderly

LIEBESTRAUM

FRANZ LISZT

Poco allegro

MELODY IN F

ANTON RUBINSTEIN

MARCH
from THE NUTCRACKER

VIOLIN

PYOTR IL'YICH TCHAIKOVSKY

MARCHE SLAVE

VIOLIN

PYOTR IL'YICH TCHAIKOVSKY

MINUET
from STRING QUINTET NO. 5

VIOLIN

LUIGI BOCCHERINI

OVERTURE
from THE NUTCRACKER

VIOLIN

PYOTR IL'YICH TCHAIKOVSKY

MORNING
from PEER GYNT

VIOLIN

EDVARD GRIEG

MINUET IN G
from ANNA MAGDALENA NOTEBOOK

JOHANN SEBASTIAN BACH

MINUET IN G

VIOLIN

LUDWIG VAN BEETHOVEN

Moderately

ODE TO JOY

from SYMPHONY NO. 9

LUDWIG VAN BEETHOVEN

Allegro

PANIS ANGELICUS

CESAR FRANCK

PIANO SONATA NO. 8: "PATHÉTIQUE"
(Second Movement Theme)

VIOLIN

LUDWIG VAN BEETHOVEN

PIANO CONCERTO IN A MINOR
(First Movement Theme)

EDVARD GRIEG

PIANO CONCERTO NO. 21
(Second Movement Theme)

WOLFGANG AMADEUS MOZART

PAVANE

VIOLIN

GABRIEL FAURÉ

PIE JESU
from REQUIEM

VIOLIN

GABRIEL FAURÉ

PIANO SONATA IN C MAJOR
(First Movement Theme)

VIOLIN

WOLFGANG AMADEUS MOZART

PRELUDE IN A MAJOR, OP. 28, NO. 7

FRÉDÉRIC CHOPIN

POLOVETZIAN DANCE
from PRINCE IGOR

VIOLIN

ALEXANDER BORODIN

PRELUDE IN C MINOR, OP. 28, NO. 20

VIOLIN

FRÉDÉRIC CHOPIN

SINFONIA
from CHRISTMAS ORATORIO

JOHANN SEBASTIAN BACH

ROMEO AND JULIET
(Love Theme)

VIOLIN

PYOTR IL'YICH TCHAIKOVSKY

POMP AND CIRCUMSTANCE

VIOLIN

EDWARD ELGAR

RONDEAU

JEAN-JOSEPH MOURET

RONDO ALLA TURCA
from PIANO SONATA NO. 11

WOLFGANG AMADEUS MOZART

SHEEP MAY SAFELY GRAZE
from CANTATA 208

VIOLIN

JOHANN SEBASTIAN BACH

Moderately

THE SORCERER'S APPRENTICE
(Theme)

PAUL DUKAS

March tempo, in 1

SPRING
from THE FOUR SEASONS
(First Movement Theme)

ANTONIO VIVALDI

SICILIANO
from FLUTE SONATA NO. 2

VIOLIN

JOHANN SEBASTIAN BACH

Andante

SKATERS WALTZ

VIOLIN

ÉMILE WALDTEUFEL

SLEEPERS, AWAKE

from CANTATA 140

VIOLIN

JOHANN SEBASTIAN BACH

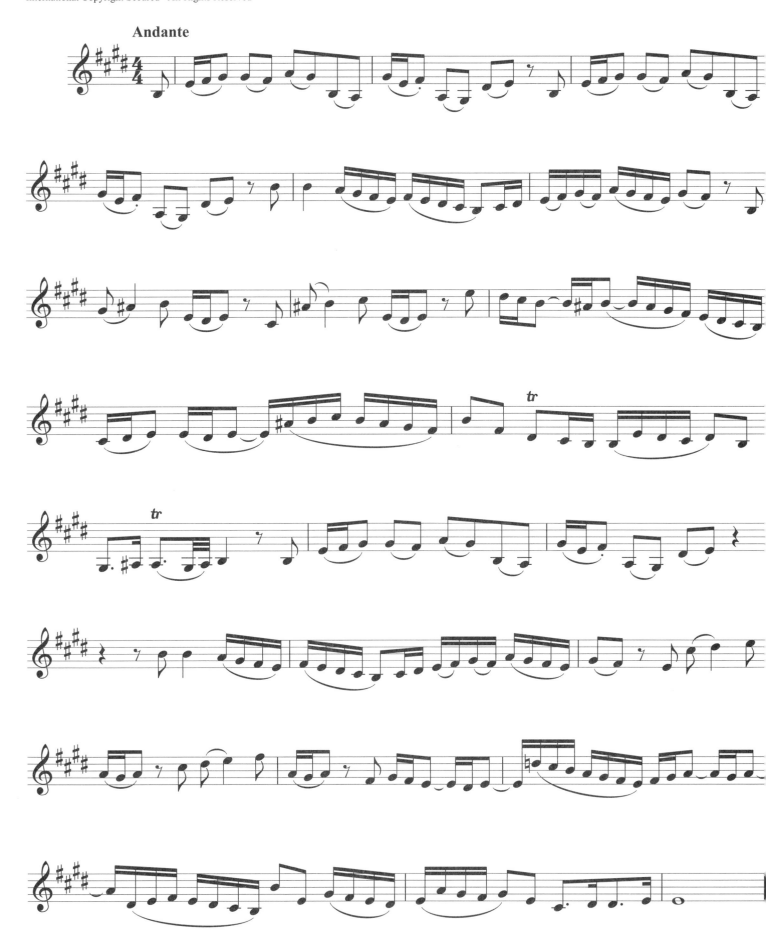

SPINNING SONG

VIOLIN

ALBERT ELLMENREICH

SWAN LAKE
(Theme)

VIOLIN

PYOTR IL'YICH TCHAIKOVSKY

Moderately

SYMPHONY NO. 5
(First Movement Theme)

VIOLIN

LUDWIG VAN BEETHOVEN

Allegro con brio

SYMPHONY NO. 1
(Fourth Movement Theme)

VIOLIN

JOHANNES BRAHMS

Allegro non troppo

SYMPHONY NO. 7
(Second Movement Theme)

LUDWIG VAN BEETHOVEN

Allegretto

SYMPHONY NO. 9

"From the New World"
(Second Movement Theme)

ANTONÍN DVOŘÁK

SYMPHONY NO. 40
(First Movement Theme)

VIOLIN

WOLFGANG AMADEUS MOZART

SYMPHONY NO. 40

(Third Movement Theme)

VIOLIN

WOLFGANG AMADEUS MOZART

Allegretto

TALES FROM THE VIENNA WOODS

VIOLIN

JOHANN STRAUSS, JR.

Waltz tempo

TO A WILD ROSE
from WOODLAND SKETCHES

VIOLIN

EDWARD MACDOWELL

Moderately, tenderly

SURPRISE SYMPHONY
(Symphony No. 94, Second Movement Theme)

VIOLIN

FRANZ JOSEPH HAYDN

Andante

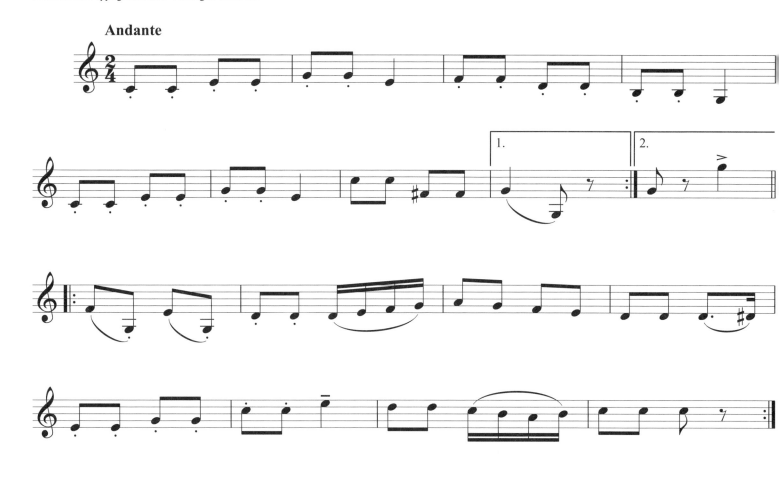

TRÄUMERAI
from SCENES FROM CHILDHOOD

ROBERT SCHUMANN

Moderately

TRUMPET TUNE

HENRY PURCELL

Moderately

TRUMPET VOLUNTARY
(Prince of Denmark's March)

VIOLIN

JEREMIAH CLARKE

WILLIAM TELL OVERTURE
(Theme)

VIOLIN

GIOACHINO ROSSINI

Allegro vivace

UNFINISHED SYMPHONY
(Symphony No. 8)
(First Movement Theme)

VIOLIN

FRANZ SCHUBERT

Allegro moderato

WALTZ OF THE FLOWERS
from THE NUTCRACKER

PYOTR IL'YICH TCHAIKOVSKY

Waltz tempo

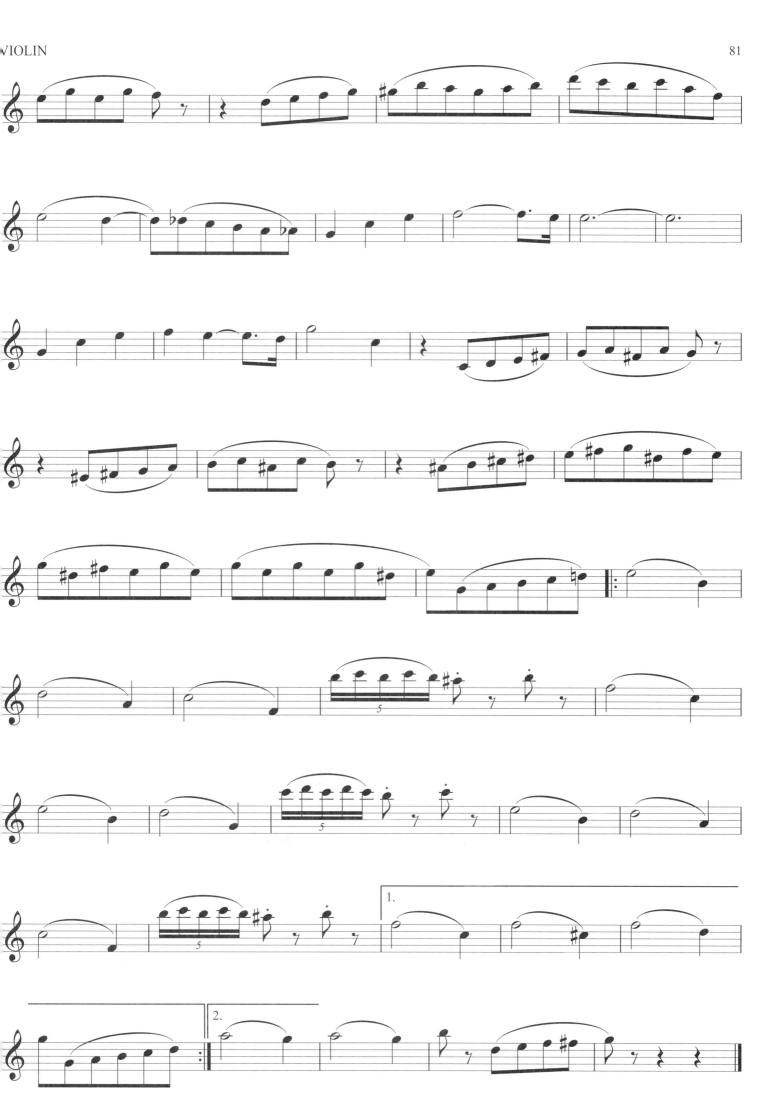

WALTZ IN C-SHARP MINOR, OP. 64, NO. 2

VIOLIN

FRÉDÉRIC CHOPIN

TOREADOR SONG
from CARMEN

VIOLIN

GEORGES BIZET

Allegro moderato

WEDDING MARCH
from A MIDSUMMER NIGHT'S DREAM

FELIX MENDELSSOHN

Allegro vivace

WHERE'ER YOU WALK
from SEMELE

VIOLIN

GEORGE FRIDERIC HANDEL

THE WILD HORSEMAN
from ALBUM FOR THE YOUNG

ROBERT SCHUMANN

D.S. al Fine
(take 1st ending)

WINTER
from THE FOUR SEASONS
(Second Movement Theme)

ANTONIO VIVALDI

101 SONGS

BIG COLLECTIONS OF FAVORITE SONGS ARRANGED FOR SOLO INSTRUMENTALISTS.

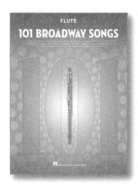

101 BROADWAY SONGS

00154199	Flute	$14.99
00154200	Clarinet	$14.99
00154201	Alto Sax	$14.99
00154202	Tenor Sax	$14.99
00154203	Trumpet	$14.99
00154204	Horn	$14.99
00154205	Trombone	$14.99
00154206	Violin	$14.99
00154207	Viola	$14.99
00154208	Cello	$14.99

101 HIT SONGS

00194561	Flute	$16.99
00197182	Clarinet	$16.99
00197183	Alto Sax	$16.99
00197184	Tenor Sax	$16.99
00197185	Trumpet	$16.99
00197186	Horn	$16.99
00197187	Trombone	$16.99
00197188	Violin	$16.99
00197189	Viola	$16.99
00197190	Cello	$16.99

101 CHRISTMAS SONGS

00278637	Flute	$14.99
00278638	Clarinet	$14.99
00278639	Alto Sax	$14.99
00278640	Tenor Sax	$14.99
00278641	Trumpet	$14.99
00278642	Horn	$14.99
00278643	Trombone	$14.99
00278644	Violin	$14.99
00278645	Viola	$14.99
00278646	Cello	$14.99

101 JAZZ SONGS

00146363	Flute	$14.99
00146364	Clarinet	$14.99
00146366	Alto Sax	$14.99
00146367	Tenor Sax	$14.99
00146368	Trumpet	$14.99
00146369	Horn	$14.99
00146370	Trombone	$14.99
00146371	Violin	$14.99
00146372	Viola	$14.99
00146373	Cello	$14.99

101 CLASSICAL THEMES

00155315	Flute	$14.99
00155317	Clarinet	$14.99
00155318	Alto Sax	$14.99
00155319	Tenor Sax	$14.99
00155320	Trumpet	$14.99
00155321	Horn	$14.99
00155322	Trombone	$14.99
00155323	Violin	$14.99
00155324	Viola	$14.99
00155325	Cello	$14.99

101 MOVIE HITS

00158087	Flute	$14.99
00158088	Clarinet	$14.99
00158089	Alto Sax	$14.99
00158090	Tenor Sax	$14.99
00158091	Trumpet	$14.99
00158092	Horn	$14.99
00158093	Trombone	$14.99
00158094	Violin	$14.99
00158095	Viola	$14.99
00158096	Cello	$14.99

101 DISNEY SONGS

00244104	Flute	$16.99
00244106	Clarinet	$16.99
00244107	Alto Sax	$16.99
00244108	Tenor Sax	$16.99
00244109	Trumpet	$16.99
00244112	Horn	$16.99
00244120	Trombone	$16.99
00244121	Violin	$16.99
00244125	Viola	$16.99
00244126	Cello	$16.99

101 POPULAR SONGS

00224722	Flute	$16.99
00224723	Clarinet	$16.99
00224724	Alto Sax	$16.99
00224725	Tenor Sax	$16.99
00224726	Trumpet	$16.99
00224727	Horn	$16.99
00224728	Trombone	$16.99
00224729	Violin	$16.99
00224730	Viola	$16.99
00224731	Cello	$16.99

HAL•LEONARD®
www.halleonard.com

Prices, contents and availability subject to change without notice.

HAL•LEONARD INSTRUMENTAL PLAY-ALONG

Your favorite songs are arranged just for solo instrumentalists with this outstanding series. Each book includes great full-accompaniment play-along audio so you can sound just like a pro! Check out **www.halleonard.com** to see all the titles available.

12 Hot Singles

Broken (lovelytheband) • Havana (Camila Cabello) • Heaven (Kane Brown) • High Hopes (Panic! At the Disco) • The Middle (Zedd, Maren Morris & Grey) • Natural (Imagine Dragons) • No Place like You (Backstreet Boys) • Shallow (Lady Gaga & Bradley Cooper) • Sucker (Jonas Brothers) • Sunflower (Post Malone & Swae Lee) • thank u, next (Ariana Grande) • Youngblood (5 Seconds of Summer).

___ 00298576	Flute	$14.99
___ 00298577	Clarinet	$14.99
___ 00298578	Alto Sax	$14.99
___ 00298579	Tenor Sax	$14.99
___ 00298580	Trumpet	$14.99
___ 00298581	Horn	$14.99
___ 00298582	Trombone	$14.99
___ 00298583	Violin	$14.99
___ 00298584	Viola	$14.99
___ 00298585	Cello	$14.99

12 Pop Hits

Believer • Can't Stop the Feeling • Despacito • It Ain't Me • Look What You Made Me Do • Million Reasons • Perfect • Send My Love (To Your New Lover) • Shape of You • Slow Hands • Too Good at Goodbyes • What About Us.

___ 00261790	Flute	$12.99
___ 00261791	Clarinet	$12.99
___ 00261792	Alto Sax	$12.99
___ 00261793	Tenor Sax	$12.99
___ 00261794	Trumpet	$12.99
___ 00261795	Horn	$12.99
___ 00261796	Trombone	$12.99
___ 00261797	Violin	$12.99
___ 00261798	Viola	$12.99
___ 00261799	Cello	$12.99

Classic Rock

(Don't Fear) The Reaper • Fortunate Son • Free Fallin' • Go Your Own Way • Jack and Diane • Money • Old Time Rock & Roll • Sweet Home Alabama • 25 or 6 to 4 • and more.

___ 00294356	Flute	$14.99
___ 00294357	Clarinet	$14.99
___ 00294358	Alto Sax	$14.99
___ 00294359	Tenor Sax	$14.99
___ 00294360	Trumpet	$14.99
___ 00294361	Horn	$14.99
___ 00294362	Trombone	$14.99
___ 00294363	Violin	$14.99
___ 00294364	Viola	$14.99
___ 00294365	Cello	$14.99

Contemporary Broadway

Defying Gravity (from Wicked) • Michael in the Bathroom (from Be More Chill) • My Shot (from Hamilton) • Seize the Day (from Newsies) • She Used to Be Mine (from Waitress) • Stupid with Love (from Mean Girls) • Waving Through a Window (from Dear Evan Hansen) • When I Grow Up (from Matilda) • and more.

___ 00298704	Flute	$14.99
___ 00298705	Clarinet	$14.99
___ 00298706	Alto Sax	$14.99
___ 00298707	Tenor Sax	$14.99
___ 00298708	Trumpet	$14.99
___ 00298709	Horn	$14.99
___ 00298710	Trombone	$14.99
___ 00298711	Violin	$14.99
___ 00298712	Viola	$14.99
___ 00298713	Cello	$14.99

Disney Movie Hits

Beauty and the Beast • Belle • Circle of Life • Cruella De Vil • Go the Distance • God Help the Outcasts • Hakuna Matata • If I Didn't Have You • Kiss the Girl • Prince Ali • When She Loved Me • A Whole New World.

___ 00841420	Flute	$12.99
___ 00841421	Clarinet	$12.99
___ 00841422	Alto Sax	$12.99
___ 00841423	Trumpet	$12.99
___ 00841424	French Horn	$12.99
___ 00841425	Trombone/Baritone	$12.99
___ 00841426	Violin	$12.99
___ 00841427	Viola	$12.99
___ 00841428	Cello	$12.99
___ 00841686	Tenor Sax	$12.99
___ 00841687	Oboe	$12.99

Disney Solos

Be Our Guest • Can You Feel the Love Tonight • Colors of the Wind • Friend like Me • Part of Your World • Under the Sea • You'll Be in My Heart • You've Got a Friend in Me • Zero to Hero • and more.

___ 00841404	Flute	$12.99
___ 00841405	Clarinet/Tenor Sax	$12.99
___ 00841406	Alto Sax	$12.99
___ 00841407	Horn	$12.99
___ 00841408	Trombone/Baritone	$12.99
___ 00841409	Trumpet	$12.99
___ 00841410	Violin	$12.99
___ 00841411	Viola	$12.99
___ 00841412	Cello	$12.99
___ 00841506	Oboe	$12.99
___ 00841553	Mallet Percussion	$12.99

Great Classical Themes

Blue Danube Waltz (Strauss) • Can Can (from Orpheus in the Underworld) (Offenbach) • Jesu, Joy of Man's Desiring (J.S. Bach) • Morning Mood (from Peer Gynt) (Grieg) • Ode to Joy (from Symphony No. 9) (Beethoven) • William Tell Overture (Rossini) • and more.

___ 00292727	Flute	$12.99
___ 00292728	Clarinet	$12.99
___ 00292729	Alto Sax	$12.99
___ 00292730	Tenor Sax	$12.99
___ 00292732	Trumpet	$12.99
___ 00292733	Horn	$12.99
___ 00292735	Trombone	$12.99
___ 00292736	Violin	$12.99
___ 00292737	Viola	$12.99
___ 00292738	Cello	$12.99

The Greatest Showman

Come Alive • From Now On • The Greatest Show • A Million Dreams • Never Enough • The Other Side • Rewrite the Stars • This Is Me • Tightrope.

___ 00277389	Flute	$14.99
___ 00277390	Clarinet	$14.99
___ 00277391	Alto Sax	$14.99
___ 00277392	Tenor Sax	$14.99
___ 00277393	Trumpet	$14.99
___ 00277394	Horn	$14.99
___ 00277395	Trombone	$14.99
___ 00277396	Violin	$14.99
___ 00277397	Viola	$14.99
___ 00277398	Cello	$14.99

Irish Favorites

Danny Boy • I Once Loved a Lass • The Little Beggarman • The Minstrel Boy • My Wild Irish Rose • The Wearing of the Green • and dozens more!

___ 00842489	Flute	$12.99
___ 00842490	Clarinet	$12.99
___ 00842491	Alto Sax	$12.99
___ 00842493	Trumpet	$12.99
___ 00842494	Horn	$12.99
___ 00842495	Trombone	$12.99
___ 00842496	Violin	$12.99
___ 00842497	Viola	$12.99
___ 00842498	Cello	$12.99

Simple Songs

All of Me • Evermore • Hallelujah • Happy • I Gotta Feeling • I'm Yours • Lava • Rolling in the Deep • Viva la Vida • You Raise Me Up • and more.

___ 00249081	Flute	$12.99
___ 00249082	Clarinet	$12.99
___ 00249083	Alto Sax	$12.99
___ 00249084	Tenor Sax	$12.99
___ 00249086	Trumpet	$12.99
___ 00249087	Horn	$12.99
___ 00249089	Trombone	$12.99
___ 00249090	Violin	$12.99
___ 00249091	Viola	$12.99
___ 00249092	Cello	$12.99
___ 00249093	Oboe	$12.99
___ 00249094	Keyboard Percussion	$12.99

Stadium Rock

Crazy Train • Don't Stop Believin' • Eye of the Tiger • Havana • Seven Nation Army • Sweet Caroline • We Are the Champions • and more.

___ 00323880	Flute	$14.99
___ 00323881	Clarinet	$14.99
___ 00323882	Alto Sax	$14.99
___ 00323883	Tenor Sax	$14.99
___ 00323884	Trumpet	$14.99
___ 00323885	Horn	$14.99
___ 00323886	Trombone	$14.99
___ 00323887	Violin	$14.99
___ 00323888	Viola	$14.99
___ 00323889	Cello	$14.99

Video Game Music

Angry Birds • Assassin's Creed III • Assassin's Creed Revelations • Battlefield 1942 • Civilization IV (Baba Yetu) • Deltarune (Don't Forget) • Elder Scrolls IV & V • Fallout® 4 • Final Fantasy VII • Full Metal Alchemist (Bratja) (Brothers) • IL-2 Sturmovik: Birds of Prey • Splinter Cell: Conviction • Undertale (Megalovania).

___ 00283877	Flute	$12.99
___ 00283878	Clarinet	$12.99
___ 00283879	Alto Sax	$12.99
___ 00283880	Tenor Sax	$12.99
___ 00283882	Trumpet	$12.99
___ 00283883	Horn	$12.99
___ 00283884	Trombone	$12.99
___ 00283885	Violin	$12.99
___ 00283886	Viola	$12.99
___ 00283887	Cello	$12.99

HAL•LEONARD®

Hal•Leonard Classical PLAY-ALONG™

MOZART

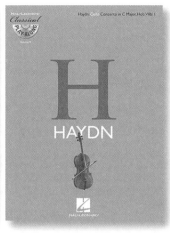
HAYDN

J.S.BACH

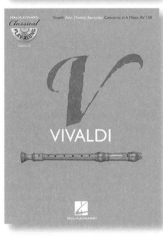
VIVALDI

BRAHMS

BEETHOVEN

The Hal Leonard Classical Play-Along™ series will help you play great classical pieces. Listen to the full performance tracks to hear how the piece sounds with an orchestra, and then play along using the accompaniment tracks. The audio CD is playable on any CD player. For PC and Mac computer users, the CD is enhanced so you can adjust the recording to any tempo without changing pitch.

1. MOZART:
FLUTE CONCERTO IN D MAJOR, K314
Book/CD Pack
00842341 Flute.......................$12.99

2. SAMMARTINI:
DESCANT (SOPRANO) RECORDER
CONCERTO IN F MAJOR
Book/CD Pack
00842342 Soprano Recorder.................$12.99

3. LOEILLET:
TREBLE (ALTO) RECORDER
SONATA IN G MAJOR, OP.1, NO.3
Book/CD Pack
00842343 Alto Recorder.......................$12.99

4. MOZART:
CLARINET CONCERTO IN A MAJOR, K622
Book/CD Pack
00842344 Clarinet...................$12.99

6. MOZART:
HORN CONCERTO IN D MAJOR, K412/514
Book/CD Pack
00842346 Horn......................$12.99

7. BACH:
VIOLIN CONCERTO IN A MINOR, BWV 1041
Book/CD Pack
00842347 Violin $12.99

8. TELEMANN:
VIOLA CONCERTO IN G MAJOR, TWV 51:G9
Book/Online Audio
00842348 Viola.......................$12.99

9. HAYDN:
CELLO CONCERTO IN C MAJOR, HOB.
VIIB: 1
Book/CD Pack
00842349 Cello.......................$12.99

10. BACH:
PIANO CONCERTO IN F MINOR, BWV 1056
Book/CD Pack
00842350 Piano......................$12.99

11. PERGOLESI:
FLUTE CONCERTO IN G MAJOR
Book/CD Pack
00842351 Flute.......................$12.99

12. BARRE:
DESCANT (SOPRANO) RECORDER
SUITE NO. 9 "DEUXIEME LIVRE" G MAJOR
Book/Online Audio
00842352 Soprano Recorder...............$12.99

14. VON WEBER:
CLARINET CONCERTO NO. 1 IN F MINOR,
OP. 73
Book/CD Pack
00842354 Clarinet $12.99

15. MOZART:
VIOLIN CONCERTO IN G MAJOR, K216
Book/CD Pack
00842355 Violin $12.99

16. BOCCHERINI:
CELLO CONCERTO IN B-FLAT MAJOR,
G482
Book/CD Pack
00842356 Cello.......................$12.99

17. MOZART:
PIANO CONCERTO IN C MAJOR, K467
Book/CD Pack
00842357 Piano.......................$12.99

18. BACH:
FLUTE SONATA IN E-FLAT MAJOR,
BWV 1031
Book/CD Pack
00842450 Flute.......................$12.99

19. BRAHMS:
CLARINET SONATA IN F MINOR, OP. 120,
NO. 1
Book/CD Pack
00842451 Clarinet.......................$12.99

20. BEETHOVEN:
TWO ROMANCES FOR VIOLIN,
OP. 40 IN G & OP. 50 IN F
Book/CD Pack
00842452 Violin $12.99

21. MOZART:
PIANO CONCERTO IN D MINOR, K466
Book/CD Pack
00842453 Piano.......................$12.99

HAL•LEONARD®

www.halleonard.com